W9-AKC-613

FROM THE EDITORS OF

ESSENCE

The OBAMAS
IN THE WHITE HOUSE
Reflections on Family, Faith & Leadership

LINDENHURST MEMORIAL LIBRARY
LINDENHURST, NEW YORK 11757

CHUCK KENNEDY/MCT/LANDOV

ESSENCE.

Editor-in-Chief: Angela Burt-Murray
Executive Editor: Dawn M. Baskerville
Creative Director: Gregory Monfries
Art Director: Kayoko Suzuki-Lange
Design Production Manager: LaToya N. Valmont
Photo Editor: Deborah Boardley
Associate Photo Editor: Tracey Woods

THE OBAMAS IN THE WHITE HOUSE:
REFLECTIONS ON FAMILY, FAITH & LEADERSHIP
SPECIAL ANNIVERSARY EDITION

Editor: Patrik Henry Bass
Design: Alisha Neumaier
Production Manager: Carina A. Rosario
Photo Editor: Helena Ashton
Research: Rachel Williams
Copy Editors: Valerie David, Hope E. Wright
Reporter: Kimberley McLeod

Content Credits:
ESSENCE acknowledges the writers
who contributed to this book:
Kimberley McLeod
Rosemarie Robotham

Speeches, addresses and remarks are located
in their entirety at Whitehouse.gov.

Publisher: Richard Fraiman
General Manager: Steven Sandonato
Executive Director, Marketing Services: Carol Pittard
Director, Retail & Special Sales: Tom Mifsud
Director, New Product Development: Peter Harper
Assistant Director, Newsstand Marketing: Laura Adam
Assistant Director, Brand Marketing: Joy Butts
Associate Counsel: Helen Wan
Brand & Licensing Manager: Alexandra Bliss
Design & Prepress Manager: Anne-Michelle Gallero
Book Production Manager: Susan Chodakiewicz

Special Thanks:
Christine Austin, Glenn Buonocore,
Jim Childs, Romeo Cifelli, Rose Cirrincione,
Fran Fitzgerald, Jacqueline Fitzgerald,
Charles Guardino, Lauren Hall, Jeffrey Ingledue,
Jennifer Jacobs, Suzanne Janso, Brynn Joyce,
Hubie Lau, Mona Li, Robert Marasco,
Amy Migliaccio, Brooke Reger, Rob Roszkowski,
Dave Rozzelle, Ilene Schreider, Adriana Tierno,
Alex Voznesenskiy, Sydney Webber

Copyright 2009
Essence Communications, Inc.
Published by Time Inc. Home
Entertainment

Time Inc.
1271 Avenue of the Americas
New York NY 10020

All rights reserved. No part of this book
may be reproduced in any form or by any
electronic or mechanical means, including
information storage and retrieval system,
without permission in writing from the
publisher, except by a reviewer, who may
quote a brief passage in a review.

ISBN 13: 978-1-60320-106-3
ISBN 10: 1-60320-106-8
Library of Congress Control Number:
2009928258

ESSENCE Books is a trademark of Time Inc.

We welcome your comments and
suggestions about ESSENCE Books.
Please write to us at:
ESSENCE Books
Attention: Book Editors
PO Box 11016
Des Moines IA 50336-1016

Front Cover: Photograph by
Pete Souza/The White House/Polaris
Back Cover: Photograph by
Jason Reed/Reuters/Landov
Jacket Inset: Photograph by
Callie Shell/Aurora Photographs

If you would like to order any of our
hardcover Collector's Edition books,
please call us at 800-327-6388
(Monday through Friday, 7:00 A.M.–8:00 P.M.,
or Saturday, 7:00 A.M.–6:00 P.M.,
Central Standard Time).

KEVIN LAMARQUE/REUTERS/CORBIS

FEBRUARY 16, 2009
Chicago, Illinois

President Obama, Mrs.
Obama, Mrs. Marian
Robinson (mother of
Mrs. Obama), Sasha
and Malia head home to
Washington, D.C. after
spending the President's
Day weekend in the
Windy City.

CONTENTS

JULY 4, 2009
Washington, D.C.

——— ∞ ———

**President Obama
and Mrs. Obama
enjoy Independence
Day fireworks in the
nation's capital.**

PETE SOUZA/MAI/LANDOV

PETE SOUZA/THE WHITE HOUSE/GETTY IMAGES

INTRODUCTION

Last spring, I went to the White House to interview First Lady Michelle Obama and her mother Marian Robinson. As we entered the East Wing, the first thing we noticed were the large color photographs of its newest residents that lined the wood-paneled hallways: the First Lady reading to students in Washington, D.C.; a behind-the-scenes moment from inauguration night, with the President and the First Lady sharing a connection in a service elevator, his jacket draped around her bare shoulders. These photographs were in stark contrast to the stately oil paintings of past presidents and first ladies that decorated other parts of the East Wing.

As the ESSENCE team waited for Mrs. Obama and her mother inside the First Lady's office, an aide pointed to a corner window and noted that you could see Marine One landing from there. The aide added that you could usually hear 11-year-old Malia and 8-year-old Sasha Obama yelling, "Daddy's home! Daddy's home!"

This single detail underscored for me just what is so special to us about the Obamas. They are, at their core, a family—parents loving one another and raising their children, even as they set an example for their girls, and for all of America, of personal responsibility, public service and private faith. Their experiences, for all the pomp and circumstance of their lives in the White House, resemble so many of our own family experiences, which have been largely invisible outside our communities. But now, with the Obamas in the White House, African-Americans finally see themselves reflected on the world's largest stage.

President Barack Obama's historic election on November 4, 2008, was a game changer for us in other ways as well. The new President's journey has certainly not been easy, nor is our Commander-in-Chief one to shrink from any challenge. As President Obama steps forward to confront economic turmoil at home and wars overseas, and the enormous task of reforming health care, ESSENCE pauses to reflect on just what his first year as the forty-fourth president of the United States has meant. In these pages, we document in stirring words and poignant images, the Obamas' incredible journey since January 20, 2009, inauguration day. We see the family at work and play; we examine their influence as they engage ordinary Americans at town hall meetings, school appearances, White House events and official trips around the world. Throughout, we include inspiring reflections from the President and the First Lady on such topics as faith and family, strength and humility, leadership and patriotism.

We hope you enjoy this record of the Obamas' extraordinary first year, and that you will embrace the promise embodied by their very presence in the White House—that we all can finally take hold of the American Dream.

Angela

Angela Burt-Murray
Editor-in-Chief

APRIL 5, 2009
Prague, Czech Republic

——❈❈❈——

Mrs. Obama watches President Obama sign the guestbook after their arrival to Prague Castle, as a part of his historic European Tour.

PART I

FAMILY

"This is one model of what a Black family can look like, but there are hundreds of others that work just as well."

—*Mrs. Obama*

JANUARY 5, 2009
Washington, D.C.

President-elect Barack Obama and Mrs. Obama get Sasha and Malia ready for their first day at Sidwell Friends School in Washington.

CALLIE SHELL/AURORA PHOTOS

❝ For me [our image] is a reminder of what is already the reality. The women in videos and the stereotypes are just not the truth of who we are as a community...But sometimes... those stereotypes define us. Sometimes we start internalizing something that is not even true. So [maybe we] can be a reminder that all you need to do is look around your own community, and you will see this same family in churches and in schools. ❞

—Mrs. Obama

MARCH 20, 2009
Washington, D.C.

⸎

President Obama hugs Mrs. Obama in the White House Red Room with Senior Advisor Valerie Jarrett looking on prior to the National Newspaper Publishers Association reception.

PETE SOUZA/THE WHITE HOUSE/POLARIS

"...This isn't an obligation.
This is a privilege to be a father.**"**
—*President Obama*

APRIL 14, 2009
Washington, D.C.

Malia walks Bo,
the Obama family's
Portuguese water
dog, as Sasha,
President Obama
and Mrs. Obama
stroll outside the
White House.

SAUL LOEB/AFP/GETTY IMAGES

❝The strength and conviction of all mothers—including those who work inside and outside the home—are inspiring. They deserve our deepest respect, admiration and appreciation.❞

—President Obama

MAY 31, 2009
New York City
—❀—

President Obama and Mrs. Obama depart early Sunday, after a Saturday dinner date and a performance of August Wilson's "Joe Turner's Come and Gone."

President Obama and Mrs. Obama deplane Air Force One after arriving for the 65th Anniversary of D-Day.

AP PHOTO/J. SCOTT APPLEWHITE; LARRY DOWNING/REUTERS/CORBIS

15

66 Government can put more cops on the streets, but only fathers can make sure that those kids aren't on the streets in the first place. Government can create good jobs, but we need fathers to train for these jobs and hold down these jobs and provide for their families... 99

—*President Obama*

MAY 12, 2009
Washington, D.C.
—⁂—

President Obama plays with Bo on the South Lawn of the White House.

PETE SOUZA/THE WHITE HOUSE/GETTY IMAGES

President Obama
reads aloud while Mrs.
Obama, Malia and
Sasha listen at the
Easter Egg Roll on the
South Lawn.

JUNE 26, 2009
Washington, D.C.

Mrs. Obama and Malia walk from the Oval Office with Bo before attending a luau (Hawaiian feast) on the South Lawn of the White House for members of Congress and their families.

LARRY DOWNING/REUTERS/LANDOV; KEVIN LAMARQUE/REUTERS/CORBIS

MAY 4, 2009
Washington, D.C.
➰

President Obama
enjoys a snack from
the buffet table
while standing
with Mrs. Obama
after the White
House's Cinco de
Mayo celebration.

SAMANTHA APPLETON/REUTERS/CORBIS; NICHOLAS KAMM/AFP/GETTY IMAGES

"I would not be standing here without the unyielding support of my best friend for the last 16 years, the rock of our family, the love of my life...Michelle Obama."

—*President Obama*

JULY 21, 2009
Washington, D.C.

President Obama listens with Malia during a country music celebration in the East Room of the White House.

> ❝ Having made it through tough times and getting to this point, having worked hard and fought hard to create something better for yourselves, having made the most of every opportunity so far that has come your way—given all that—just think, you should have more confidence, not less...And no matter what happens, I want you to remember that you already have one of the greatest gifts as a young person that you can ever have. You have a parent or an adult in your life who believes in you. ❞

—*Mrs. Obama*

FEBRUARY 22, 2009
Washington, D.C.

⟞⟝

Mrs. Obama touches up the president before receiving guests at the Governors' Ball at the White House.

CALLIE SHELL/AURORA PHOTOS

23

"There is no substitute for the bond of love between mother and child, and nothing is more worthy of reverence."

—*President Obama*

PETE SOUZA/THE WHITE HOUSE

Mrs. Obama, with Malia and Sasha, sled in the snow on the South Lawn of the White House.

66 ...Nothing is more fun than being a father. My kids aren't teenagers yet, so I don't know whether that will maintain itself. But right now the greatest joy I get is just hanging out with the girls and talking to them and watching them grow and succeed. 99 —*President Obama*

FEBRUARY 1, 2009
Washington, D.C.
⟶⟶⟶⟶⟶

President Obama and Mrs. Obama wear 3-D glasses while watching Super Bowl XLIII, Arizona Cardinals vs. Pittsburgh Steelers, at the Super Bowl Party in the family theater of the White House. Guests included family, friends, staff members and bipartisan members of Congress.

Malia reads the back of a card featuring Bo, while helping to fill 15,000 backpacks for children of military servicemen and women.

PETE SOUZA/THE WHITE HOUSE/POLARIS; CHIP SOMODEVILLA/GETTY IMAGES

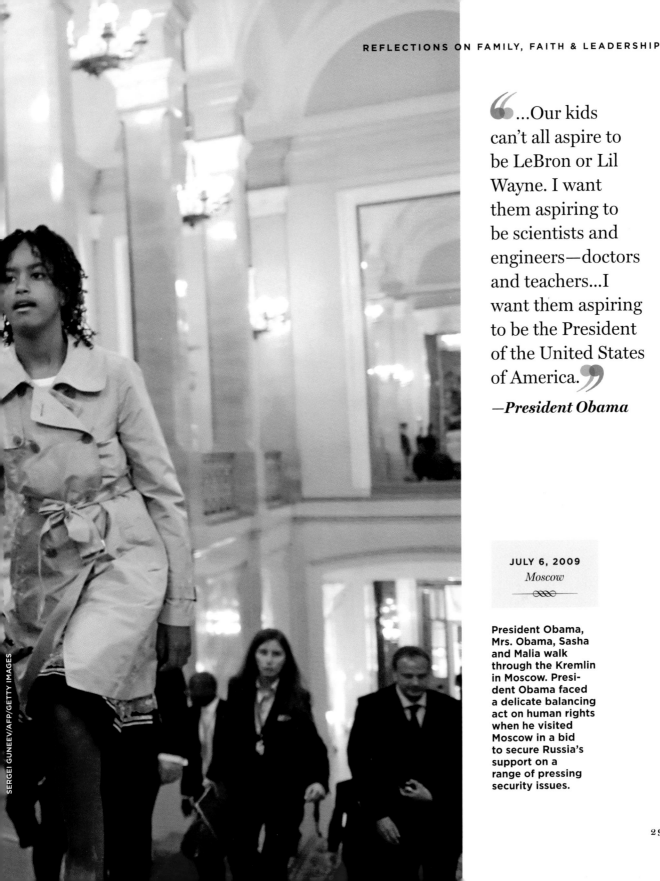

SERGEI GUNEEV/AFP/GETTY IMAGES

66...Our kids can't all aspire to be LeBron or Lil Wayne. I want them aspiring to be scientists and engineers—doctors and teachers...I want them aspiring to be the President of the United States of America. 99

—*President Obama*

JULY 6, 2009
Moscow
—∞∞∞—

President Obama, Mrs. Obama, Sasha and Malia walk through the Kremlin in Moscow. President Obama faced a delicate balancing act on human rights when he visited Moscow in a bid to secure Russia's support on a range of pressing security issues.

66 When my daughters were born, I made a pledge to them, that I would do everything I could to give them some things I didn't have. And I decided that if I could be one thing in life, it would be to be a good father...It's not always about succeeding; it's about always trying. 99

—*President Obama*

FEBRUARY 8, 2009
Washington, D.C.

Sasha stops by to say hello to her dad in the Oval Office of the White House.

CALLIE SHELL/AURORA PHOTOS

BRENDAN SMIALOWSKI/POOL/CORBIS; ZBIGNIEW BZDAK/MCT/LANDOV

MAY 16, 2009
Washington, D.C.

President Obama cheers after Sasha's soccer team scores a point during a game.

" I had a heroic mom and wonderful grandparents who helped raise me and my sister...But despite all their extraordinary love and attention, that doesn't mean that I didn't feel my father's absence. " —*President Obama*

NOVEMBER 10, 2008
Chicago, Illinois

President-elect Barack Obama takes Malia and Sasha to their final days of class at the University of Chicago Lab School in Chicago, before moving to the White House.

There is a sense of security that allows you to take risks. People think that it comes from...generations of access and success, but it doesn't. The security of your parents' love really gives you the foundation to think you can fly. And then you do. —*Mrs. Obama*

JANUARY 5, 2009
Bethesda, Maryland

Mrs. Obama and Sasha are escorted by a full security detail as Sasha enters Sidwell Friends School for her first day of school.

PAUL J. RICHARDS/AFP/GETTY IMAGES; JIM YOUNG/REUTERS/LANDOV

APRIL 13, 2009
Washington, D.C.

Mrs. Obama walks
with Malia during the
White House's annual
Easter Egg Roll.

APRIL 13, 2009
Washington, D.C.

President Obama, Sasha, Mrs. Obama, Mrs. Robinson and Malia wave from the Truman Balcony of the White House before the start of the 2009 Easter Egg Roll.

LARRY DOWNING/REUTERS/CORBIS

"We need fathers to be involved in their kids' lives not just when it's easy —not just during the afternoons in the park or at the zoo, when it's all fun and games—but when it's hard, when young people are struggling, and there aren't any quick fixes or easy answers..."

—*President Obama*

APRIL 13, 2009
Washington, D.C.

Malia and Sasha listen to their father read a story at the 2009 Easter Egg Roll.

LARRY DOWNING/REUTERS/CORBIS

PETE SOUZA/THE WHITE HOUSE/CORBIS

FEBRUARY 22, 2009

Washington, D.C.

President Obama and Mrs. Obama dance while the band Earth, Wind & Fire performs at the Governors' Ball in the State Dining Room of the White House.

Sasha skips her
way out of the
White House to
board Marine One.

> 66 Balancing work and family is no easy task, but mothers across our nation meet this challenge each day, often without recognition for their hard work and dedication. 99
>
> —*President Obama*

JULY 4, 2009
Washington, D.C.

President Obama kisses Malia after delivering a speech during an event to celebrate Independence Day and to honor military heroes and their families on the South Lawn at the White House.

AP PHOTO/ALEX BRANDON; JEWEL SAMAD/AFP/GETTY IMAGES

❝ I want you all to open yourselves up to the entire college experience. Make new friends. Learn about other people's cultures and experiences... Learn a language. Read lots of books. That's one thing Barack Obama does all the time. He reads everything. Travel. Spend a semester abroad. You'll have those opportunities. And challenge your mind to embrace the diversity of the world that we live in, because this world is so much smaller than this school, than this city, than the campus that you'll be on. This world is big. **❞**

—Mrs. Obama

JULY 11, 2009
Accra, Ghana

President Obama walks with Mrs. Obama, Malia and Sasha during a departure ceremony in Ghana. The visit marks Obama's first to sub-Saharan Africa as president.

AP PHOTO/CHARLES DHARAPAK

JASON REED/REUTERS/LANDOV

❝ No one has written your destiny for you. Your destiny is in your hands—you cannot forget that. That's what we have to teach all of our children. No excuses. No excuses. **❞**

—*President Obama*

JULY 10, 2009
Accra, Ghana

President Obama, Malia, Sasha and Mrs. Obama arrive in Accra, Ghana, where he was given a hero's welcome.

66 If we want our children to succeed in life, we need fathers to step up. We need fathers to understand that their work doesn't end with conception—that what truly makes a man a father is the ability to raise a child and invest in that child. 99 —*President Obama*

FEBRUARY 2, 2009
Washington, D.C.

President Obama shares a tender moment with Malia and Sasha while kissing Mrs. Obama in a private study near the Oval Office.

PETE SOUZA/THE WHITE HOUSE/THE WHITE HOUSE/CNP/CORBIS; PETE SOUZA/THE WHITE HOUSE

MARCH 5, 2009
Washington, D.C.

President Obama
walks along the
Colonnade with
Malia and Sasha.

PART II

FAITH & SERVICE

"Our nation's story begins with a call to volunteer...patriots rallied to serve a cause greater than themselves. As the beneficiaries of this legacy, we possess an obligation to volunteer and serve our fellow citizens with similar selflessness and optimism."
—*President Obama*

AP PHOTO/MANUEL BALCE CENETA

MAY 13, 2009
Washington, D.C.

Mrs. Obama gives
encouragement
to third-grade
students at Ferebee
Hope Community
School in southeast
Washington.

❝ Americans keep this proud tradition alive every day across our country. They are protecting us in uniform, feeding the hungry, tutoring children, comforting seniors and reaching out to veterans. They are providing critical support to schools, shelters, hospitals and nursing homes, through faith-based and community organizations, at home and abroad. Volunteers change lives and strengthen our nation and our world. **❞**

—*President Obama*

MAY 22, 2009
*Annapolis,
Maryland*

President Obama greets a graduate of the 2009 U.S. Naval Academy class where the president was the commencement speaker.

66 Every American who volunteers can become an integral part of a school, a hospital or a neighborhood. Those who give of their time also join our nation's proud history of service and help preserve this tradition for generations ahead. 99 —*President Obama*

FEBRUARY 3, 2009
Washington, D.C.

Mrs. Obama and the president celebrate time away from the White House during a visit to the Capital City Public Charter School.

DOUG MILLS/THE NEW YORK TIMES/REDUX; AP PHOTO/MANUEL

JULY 22, 2009
Washington, D.C.
〜〜〜

Mrs. Marian Robinson reads to children gathered outside the Education Department in Washington during a "Read to The Top!" summer reading program.

President Obama
and Mrs. Obama visit
La General Hospital
during their historic
visit to Accra.

AP PHOTO/HARAZ N. GHANBARI

" ...We must find a way to reconcile our ever-shrinking world with its ever-growing... diversity of thought, diversity of culture and diversity of belief. In short, we must find a way to live together as one human family. **"**

—President Obama

APRIL 21, 2009
Washington, D.C.

Mrs. Obama participates in a tree-planting event at the Kenilworth Park and Aquatic Gardens in Washington, with the Student Conservation Association, a partner with the AmeriCorps organization.

MARTIN H. SIMON/GETTY IMAGES

STAN HONDA/AFP/GETTY IMAGES; AP PHOTO/L'OSSERVATORE ROMANO

MAY 18, 2009
New York City
⟨⟨⟨

**Mrs. Obama hugs
a student at the
Metropolitan
Museum of Art.**

"...When people set aside their differences, even for a moment, to work in common effort toward a common goal; when they struggle together and sacrifice together, and learn from one another...all things are possible."

—*President Obama*

JULY 10, 2009
Rome, Italy

Mrs. Obama takes in a painting with a guide during a visit in the Sistine Chapel at The Vatican.

"...When I talk to kids everywhere, I remind them that they're never too young to serve, that they're never too small to do something big... —**Mrs. Obama**

MARCH 12, 2009
Fayetteville, North Carolina

Mrs. Obama reads "The Cat in the Hat" by Dr. Seuss to children at the Prager Child Development Center for military families inside Ft. Bragg.

MARCH 5, 2009
Washington, D.C.
〰

Mrs. Obama
volunteers at
Miriam's Kitchen
in Washington.
The center
provides meals,
case management
services and
housing support
to nearly 250
men and women.

ALEX WONG/GETTY IMAGES

"...my father and my mother were unconditionally rooting for me. And kids need that too. Looking back that played such a huge role in building confidence in me and my brother. Whether we succeeded or failed, we had two people who lifted us up..."

—*Mrs. Obama*

MAY 29, 2009
Washington, D.C.

Mrs. Obama speaks to students during a visit to Bancroft Elementary School. The students helped with the White House Kitchen Garden events.

"...The ultimate irony of faith is that it necessarily admits doubt...This doubt should not push away our faith. But it should humble us. It should temper our passions, cause us to be wary of too much self-righteousness. **"**

—President Obama

JULY 7, 2009
Moscow

Mrs. Obama meets nurses during her visit to St. Dmitry Nursing College of Sisters of Mercy.

MAXIM SHEMETOV/ITAR-TASS/LANDOV; MARTIN H. SIMON/UPI/LANDOV

APRIL 12, 2009
Washington, D.C.

President Obama
and Mrs. Obama
depart St. John's
Episcopal Church
following the Easter
Sunday service
in Washington.

Mrs. Obama delivers remarks for the Corporation for National & Community Service at the Ronald Reagan Building.

AP PHOTO/PABLO MARTINEZ MONSIVAIS; JEWEL SAMAD/AFP/GETTY IMAGES

Corporation for
NATIONAL &
COMMUNITY
SERVICE ★★★

When somebody told me that I couldn't do something or be something, that just gave me a greater challenge to prove them wrong. And with every little challenge like that, and every little success, I gained more confidence.

—*Mrs. Obama*

JUNE 16, 2009
Washington, D.C.

Mrs. Obama and students from Bancroft Elementary School harvest vegetables in the White House Kitchen Garden.

66It's not the money you make or the degree that you have, but in many ways it's the choice that you make to be an active and involved and responsible citizen. 99

—*Mrs. Obama*

APRIL 28, 2009
Washington, D.C.

Mrs. Obama and
Nancy Pelosi, Speaker
of the House of
Representatives,
applaud the unveiling
of a bust of
Sojourner Truth.

JASON REED/REUTERS/LANDOV

PART III

LEADERSHIP

"I believe it is not in our character, the American character, to follow. It's our character to lead. And it is time for us to lead once again."

—President Obama

APRIL 24, 2009
Washington, D.C.

President Obama speaks about his plans for higher education in the Diplomatic Room of the White House.

AUDE GUERRUCCI/UPI/LANDOV

DARIO PIGNATELLI/POLARIS

  ❝ I know that years from now we will look back on this time, at this moment, and say… that's when the American people came together to reclaim their future—to write the next great chapter of the American story. ❞

—*President Obama*

President Obama and French President Nicolas Sarkozy attend the G8 Summit.

MARCH 17, 2009
Washington, D.C.

President Obama reviews a document in the Oval Office of the White House as Chief of Staff Rahm Emanuel and Press Secretary Robert Gibbs talk in the background.

CALLIE SHELL/AURORA PHOTOS

GALLIE SHELL/AURORA PHOTOS

"...Developed countries like my own have an historic responsibility to take the lead. We have the much larger carbon footprint... and I know that in the past, the United States has sometimes fallen short...So, let me be clear: Those days are over."

—*President Obama*

APRIL 5, 2009
Prague, Czech Republic

President Obama addresses the crowd in the Square in Prague.

79

66 The days of Washington dragging its heels are over. My administration will not deny facts, we will be guided by them. 99 *—President Obama*

FEBRUARY 4, 2009
Washington, D.C.

President Obama signs the State Children's Health Insurance Program bill in the East Room.

ALEXIS C. GLENN/UPI/LANDOV

" Now is the time to meet the challenge at this crossroad of history by choosing a future that is safer for our country, prosperous for our planet and sustainable. "

—President Obama

FEBRUARY 24, 2009
Washington, D.C.

President Obama is applauded during his eagerly anticipated first address to a joint session of Congress at the Capitol in Washington.

SAUL LOEB/AFP/GETTY IMAGES; AP PHOTO/REMY DE LA MAUVINIERE

JUNE 6, 2009
Normandy, France

President Obama, Prince Charles, British Prime Minister Gordon Brown, Canada's Prime Minister Stephen Harper and French President Nicolas Sarkozy celebrate the 65th anniversary of D-Day.

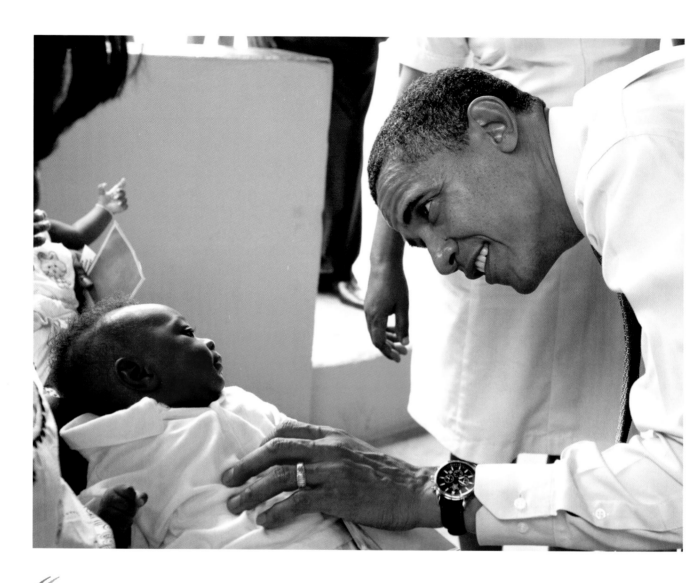

66 I...have the blood of Africa within me, and my family's—
my family's own story encompasses both the tragedies and
triumphs of the larger African story. 99 —*President Obama*

JULY 11, 2009
Accra, Ghana

**President Obama
tickles a baby dur-
ing his tour of La
General Hospital.**

66 To be able to come back here in celebration with the people of Ghana of the extraordinary progress that we've made because of the courage of so many...to abolish slavery is a source of hope.99

—*President Obama*

Malia, Mrs. Obama, Sasha, Mrs. Robinson and President Obama take a walk during a guided tour of Cape Coast Castle, a former slavery outpost.

SAUL LOEB/AFP/GETTY IMAGES

85

"...Women play leadership roles in the health and education of our families, in our fields, our factories, our classrooms, our laboratories and our boardrooms. With or without awards...women have taught us about hope, about courage and about opportunity."

—*President Obama*

JUNE 4, 2009
Cairo, Egypt

President Obama, Senior Advisor Valerie Jarrett and Secretary of State Hillary Clinton tour in Cairo.

PETE SOUZA/THE WHITE HOUSE/POLARIS

"...No matter how bitter the rod, how stony the road, we have always persevered. We have not faltered, nor have we grown weary. As Americans, we have demanded, and strived for, and shaped a better destiny. And that is what we are called on to do once more."

—President Obama

JULY 30, 2009
Washington, D.C.

President Obama shares a
beer with Harvard University
Professor Henry Louis
Gates, Jr., and Cambridge,
Massachusetts Police Sgt.
James Crowley in the Rose
Garden at the White House.
President Obama encour-
aged both men to have a
thoughtful conversation on
race after Crowley arrested
Gates for disorderly conduct
outside his home, following
a 911 call reporting
a break-in at Gates' house.

PETE SOUZA/THE WHITE HOUSE/GETTY IMAGES

APRIL 7, 2009
Baghdad, Iraq

U.S. Military person-
nel greet President
Obama during a
surprise visit to
"Camp Victory."

CALLIE SHELL/AURORA PHOTOS

“...It turns out that young people are incredibly resilient. It doesn't take that much. All it takes is somebody to put a hand on them and say, 'You know what? You're important. And I'm listening to you.'”

—*President Obama*

MAY 8, 2009
Washington, D.C.

President Obama plays with the son of a White House staffer during a visit to the Oval Office.

PETE SOUZA/MAI/LANDOV

JULY 4, 2009
Washington, D.C.
⸎

**President Obama
and Mrs. Obama
greet military
families at the
White House.**

"We can either shape our future, or we can let events shape it for us…That's the responsibility of our generation, that must be our legacy for generations to come." —*President Obama*

PETE SOUZA/MAI/LANDOV

66...We have lived through an era where too often short-term gains were prized over long-term prosperity, where we failed to look beyond the next payment, the next quarter or the next election. 99 —*President Obama*

FEBRUARY 26, 2009
Washington, D.C.

President Obama and his personal aide Reggie Love share a laugh after an event in the Eisenhower Executive Office Building of the White House.

CALLIE SHELL/AURORA PHOTOS ; AP PHOTO/PABLO MARTINEZ MONSIVAIS

JULY 1, 2009
Annandale, Virginia

President Obama, with
Senior Advisor Valerie
Jarrett, take questions
during a discussion
on health care at
Northern Virginia
Community College.

SAUL LOEB/AFP/GETTY IMAGES

JULY 11, 2009
Accra, Ghana

President Obama reviews an honor guard at the Presidential Castle in Accra, Ghana. President Obama, who addressed parliament, said before the trip that he had chosen Ghana as his first visit to sub-Saharan Africa because it was an example of a functioning democracy in a conflict-scarred continent.

SEAL OF THE PRESIDENT OF THE UNITED STATES

APRIL 19, 2009
Washington, D.C.

President Obama
arrives by
Marine One on the
South Lawn of the
White House, after
returning from
the Fifth Summit
of the Americas
held in Trinidad
and Tobago.

AUDE GUERRUCCI/AFP/GETTY IMAGES/PETE SOUZA/AA/LANDOV

❝...I think everybody understands this is an extraordinary moment, one in which we are called upon not just to restore fiscal responsibility, but to once again live up to the broader responsibilities we have to one another... We have the capacity to change, and to grow, and to solve even our toughest of problems.❞ *—President Obama*

JANUARY 27, 2009
Washington, D.C.

President Obama reaches across the aisle while attending a lunch with Senate Republicans on Capitol Hill.

"❝ There's one rule that lies at the heart of every religion—That we do unto others as we would have them do unto us. This truth transcends nations and peoples—a belief that isn't new; that isn't black or white or brown; that isn't Christian or Muslim or Jew.❞

—*President Obama*

JUNE 4, 2009
Cairo, Egypt

President Obama tours the Pyramids and Sphinx with Secretary General of the Egyptian Supreme Council of Antiquities Zahi Hawass (left), Senior Advisor David Axelrod (right) and Chief of Staff Rahm Emanuel (far right).

PETE SOUZA/THE WHITE HOUSE/POLARIS

66 Each side will continue to make its case to the public with passion and conviction. But surely we can do so without reducing those with differing views to caricature. 99

—President Obama

APRIL 5, 2009
*Prague, Czech
Republic*

President Obama,
with Mrs. Obama,
waves before a
speech in Prague.
President Obama
laid out an ambi-
tious plan to rid
the world of atomic
weapons in Prague,
evoking his suc-
cessful election
campaign slogan
of "Yes, we can"
to call for world
action to face up to
the nuclear threat.

RALF HIRSCHBERGER/EPA/CORBIS; SAUL LOEB/AFP/GETTY IMAGES

JULY 10, 2009
Rome, Italy

Pope Benedict XVI poses with President Obama and Mrs. Obama during an audience at The Vatican. President Obama was meeting Pope Benedict XVI for the first time, with their talks covering areas of agreement such as foreign policy.

"...I am convinced that in order to move forward, we must say openly to each other the things we hold in our hearts and that too often are said only behind closed doors. There must be a sustained effort to listen to each other; to learn from each other; to respect one another." *—President Obama*

APRIL 1, 2009
London
⁕

President Obama and Mrs. Obama visit with Queen Elizabeth II and Prince Philip, Duke of Edinburgh, at Buckingham Palace.

JOHN STILLWELL/REUTERS/CORBIS;
DANIEL HAMBURY/REUTERS/CORBIS

APRIL 1, 2009
London

Mrs. Obama gently
touches Queen
Elizabeth II during
a G-20 leaders
reception at Buck-
ingham Palace.

MAY 7, 2009
Washington, D.C.

President Obama greets New York Mayor Michael Bloomberg, Reverend Al Sharpton and former speaker of the House Newt Gingrich to discuss education reform.

66 ...When you serve, it doesn't just improve your community; it makes you a part of your community. It breaks down walls. It fosters cooperation. 99

—*President Obama*

APRIL 1, 2009
London

President Obama shakes the hand of a British police officer outside 10 Downing Street.

"...Making our economy work means making sure it works for everybody; that there are no second-class citizens in our workplaces."

—*President Obama*

JANUARY 29, 2009
Washington, D.C.

President Obama signs the Lilly Ledbetter bill in the East Room.

AUDE GUERRUCCI/POLARIS

SPEECHES

From the beginning, these founders understood how change would come—just as King and all the civil rights giants did later. They understood that unjust laws needed to be overturned; that legislation needed to be passed; and that Presidents needed to be pressured into action.

President Obama delivers a rousing speech at the NAACP's centennial celebration in New York, July 16, 2009.

AP PHOTO/HARAZ N. GHANBARI

"WE WILL REBUILD, WE WILL RECOVER"

On February 24, 2009, President Obama illuminated his strategy to revive the economy and "to build a new foundation for lasting prosperity" in his first address to a joint session of Congress

I've come here tonight not only to address the distinguished men and women in this great chamber, but to speak frankly and directly to the men and women who sent us here.

I know that for many Americans watching right now, the state of our economy is a concern that rises above all others. And rightly so. If you haven't been personally affected by this recession, you probably know someone who has—a friend; a neighbor; a member of your family. You don't need to hear another list of statistics to know that our economy is in crisis, because you live it every day. It's the worry you wake up with and the source of sleepless nights. It's the job you thought you'd retire from but now have lost; the business you built your dreams upon that's now hanging by a thread; the college acceptance letter your child had to put back in the envelope. The impact of this recession is real, and it is everywhere.

But while our economy may be weakened and our confidence shaken; though we are living through difficult and uncertain times, tonight I want every American to know this: We will rebuild, we will recover and the United States of America will emerge stronger than before.

The weight of this crisis will not determine the destiny of this nation. The answers to our problems don't lie beyond our reach. They exist in our laboratories and universities; in our fields and our factories; in the imaginations of our entrepreneurs and the pride of the hardest-working people on Earth. Those qualities that have made America the greatest force of progress and prosperity in human history we still possess in ample measure. What is required now is for this country to pull together, confront boldly the challenges we face and take responsibility for our future once more.

Now, if we're honest with ourselves, we'll admit that for too long, we have not always met these responsibilities—as a government or as a people. I say this not to lay blame or look backwards, but because it is only by understanding how we arrived at this moment that we'll be able to lift ourselves out of this predicament.

The fact is, our economy did not fall into decline overnight. Nor did all of our problems begin when the housing market collapsed or the stock market sank. We have known for decades that our survival depends on finding new sources of energy. Yet we import more oil today than ever before. The cost of health care eats up more and more of our savings each year, yet we keep delaying reform. Our children will compete for jobs in a global economy that too many of our schools do not prepare them for. And though all these challenges went unsolved, we still managed to spend more money and pile up more debt, both as individuals and through our government, than ever before.

In other words, we have lived through an era where too often, short-term gains were prized over long-term prosperity; where we failed to look beyond the next payment, the next quarter or the next election. A surplus became an excuse to transfer wealth to the wealthy instead of an opportunity to invest in our future. Regulations were gutted for the sake of a quick profit at the expense of a healthy market. People bought homes they knew they couldn't afford from banks and lenders who pushed those bad loans anyway. And all the while, critical debates and difficult decisions were put off for some other time on some other day.

Well that day of reckoning has arrived, and the time to take charge of our future is here. Now is the time to act boldly and wisely—to not only revive this economy, but to build a new foundation for lasting prosperity. Now is the time to jump-start job creation, restart lending and invest in areas like energy, health care and education that will grow our economy, even as we make hard choices to bring our deficit down. That is what my economic agenda is designed to do, and that's what I'd like to talk to you about tonight.

It's an agenda that begins with jobs.

As soon as I took office, I asked this Congress to send me a recovery plan by President's Day that would put people back to work and put money in their pockets. Not because I believe in bigger government—I don't. Not because I'm not mindful of the massive debt we've inherited—I am. I called for action because the failure to do so would have cost more jobs and caused more hardships. In fact, a failure to act would have worsened our long-term deficit by assuring weak economic growth for years. That's why I pushed for quick action. And tonight, I am grateful that this Congress delivered, and pleased to say that the American Recovery and Reinvestment Act is now law.

Over the next two years, this plan will save or create 3.5 million jobs. More than 90% of these jobs will be in the private sector—jobs rebuilding our roads and bridges; constructing wind turbines and solar panels; laying broadband and expanding mass transit.

Because of this plan, there are teachers who can now keep their jobs and educate our kids. Health care professionals can continue caring for our sick. There are 57 police officers who are still on the streets of Minneapolis tonight because this plan prevented the layoffs their department was about to make. Because of this plan, 95% of the working households in America will receive a tax cut—a tax cut that you will see in your paychecks beginning on April 1st.

Because of this plan, families who are struggling to pay tuition costs will receive a $2,500 tax credit for all four years of college. And Americans who have lost their jobs in this recession will be able to receive extended unemployment benefits and continued health care coverage to help them weather this storm.

I know there are some in this chamber and watching at home who are skeptical of whether this plan will work. I understand that skepticism. Here in Washington, we've all seen how quickly good intentions can turn into broken promises and wasteful spending. And with a plan of this scale comes enormous responsibility to get it right.

That is why I have asked Vice President Biden to lead a tough, unprecedented oversight effort—because nobody messes with Joe. I have told each member of my Cabinet, as well as mayors and governors across the country, that they will be held accountable by me and the American people for every dollar they spend. I have appointed a proven and aggressive Inspector General to ferret out any and all cases of waste and fraud. And we have created a new Web site called recovery.gov so that every American can find out how and where their money is being spent.

So the recovery plan we passed is the first step in getting our economy back on track. But it is just the first step. Because even if we manage this plan flawlessly, there will be no real recovery unless we clean up the credit crisis that has severely weakened our financial system.

I want to speak plainly and candidly about this issue tonight, because every American should know that it directly affects you and your family's well-being. You should also know that the money you've deposited in banks across the country is safe; your insurance is secure; and you can rely on the continued operation of our financial system. That is not the source of concern.

The concern is that if we do not restart lending in this country, our recovery will be choked off before it even begins.

You see, the flow of credit is the lifeblood of our economy. The ability to get a loan is how you finance the purchase of everything from a home to a car to a college education; how stores stock their shelves, farms buy equipment and businesses make payroll.

But credit has stopped flowing the way it should. Too many bad loans from the housing crisis have made their way onto the books of too many banks. With so much debt and so little confidence, these banks are now fearful of lending out any more money to households, to businesses or to each other. When there is no lending, families can't afford to buy homes or cars. So businesses are forced to make layoffs. Our economy suffers even more, and credit dries up even further.

That is why this administration is moving swiftly and aggressively to break this destructive cycle, restore confidence and restart lending.

We will do so in several ways. First, we are creating a new lending fund that represents the largest effort ever to help provide auto loans, college loans and small business loans to the consumers and entrepreneurs who keep this economy running.

Second, we have launched a housing plan that will help responsible families facing the threat of foreclosure lower their monthly payments and refinance their mortgages. It's a plan that won't help speculators or that neighbor down the street who bought a house he could never hope to afford, but it will help millions of Americans who are struggling with declining home values—Americans who will now be able to take advantage of the lower interest rates that this plan has already helped bring about. In fact, the average family who refinances today can save nearly $2,000 per year on their mortgage.

Third, we will act with the full force of the federal government to ensure that the major banks that Americans depend on have enough confidence and enough money to lend even in more difficult times. And when we learn that a major bank has serious problems, we will hold accountable those responsible, force the necessary adjustments, provide the support to clean up their balance sheets, and assure the continuity of a strong, viable institution that can serve our people and our economy.

I understand that on any given day, Wall Street may be more comforted by an approach that gives banks bailouts with no strings attached, and that holds nobody accountable for their reckless decisions. But such an approach won't solve the problem. And our goal is to quicken the day when we restart lending to the American people and American business and end this crisis once and for all.

I intend to hold these banks fully accountable for the assistance they receive, and this time, they will have to clearly demonstrate how taxpayer dollars result in more lending for the American taxpayer. This time, CEOs won't be able to use taxpayer money to pad their paychecks or buy fancy drapes or disappear on a private jet. Those days are over.

Still, this plan will require significant resources from the federal government—and yes, probably more than we've already set aside. But while the cost of action will be great, I can assure you that the cost of inaction will be far greater, for it could result in an economy that sputters along for not months or years, but perhaps a decade. That would be worse for our deficit, worse for business, worse for you and worse for the next generation. And I refuse to let that happen.

I understand that when the last administration asked this Congress to provide assistance for struggling banks, Democrats and Republicans alike were infuriated by the mismanagement and results that followed. So were the American taxpayers. So was I.

So I know how unpopular it is to be seen as helping banks right now, especially when everyone is suffering in part from their bad decisions. I promise you—I get it.

But I also know that in a time of crisis, we cannot afford to govern out of anger, or yield to the politics of the moment. My job—our job—is to solve the problem. Our job is to govern with a sense of responsibility. I will not spend a single penny for the purpose of rewarding a single Wall Street executive, but I will do whatever it takes to help the small business that can't pay its workers or the family that has saved and still can't get a mortgage.

That's what this is about. It's not about helping banks—it's about helping people. Because when credit is available again, that young family can finally buy a new home. And then some company will hire workers to build it. And then those workers will have money to spend, and if they can get a loan too, maybe they'll finally buy that car, or open their own business. Investors will return to the market, and American families will see their retirement secured once more. Slowly, but surely, confidence will return, and our economy will recover.

So I ask this Congress to join me in doing whatever proves necessary. Because we cannot consign our nation to an open-ended recession. And to ensure that a crisis of this magnitude never happens again,

I ask Congress to move quickly on legislation that will finally reform our outdated regulatory system. It is time to put in place tough, new common-sense rules of the road so that our financial market rewards drive and innovation, and punishes shortcuts and abuse.

The recovery plan and the financial stability plan are the immediate steps we're taking to revive our economy in the short-term. But the only way to fully restore America's economic strength is to make the long-term investments that will lead to new jobs, new industries and a renewed ability to compete with the rest of the world. The only way this century will be another American century is if we confront at last the price of our dependence on oil and the high cost of health care; the schools that aren't preparing our children and the mountain of debt they stand to inherit. That is our responsibility.

In the next few days, I will submit a budget to Congress. So often, we have come to view these documents as simply numbers on a page or laundry lists of programs. I see this document differently. I see it as a vision for America—as a blueprint for our future.

My budget does not attempt to solve every problem or address every issue. It reflects the stark reality of what we've inherited—a trillion dollar deficit, a financial crisis and a costly recession.

Given these realities, everyone in this chamber—Democrats and Republicans—will have to sacrifice some worthy priorities for which there are no dollars. And that includes me.

But that does not mean we can afford to ignore our long-term challenges. I reject the view that says our problems will simply take care of themselves; that says government has no role in laying the foundation for our common prosperity.

For history tells a different story. History reminds us that at every moment of economic upheaval and transformation, this nation has responded with bold action and big ideas. In the midst of civil war, we laid railroad tracks from one coast to another that spurred commerce and industry. From the turmoil of the Industrial Revolution came a system of public high schools that prepared our citizens for a new age. In the wake of war and depression, the GI Bill sent a generation to college and created the largest middle-class in history. And a twilight struggle for freedom led to a nation of highways, an American on the moon and an explosion of technology that still shapes our world.

In each case, government didn't supplant private enterprise; it catalyzed private enterprise. It created the conditions for thousands of entrepreneurs and new businesses to adapt and to thrive.

We are a nation that has seen promise amid peril, and claimed opportunity from ordeal. Now we must be that nation again. That is why, even as it cuts back on the programs we don't need, the budget I

AP PHOTO/CHARLES DHARAPAK

President Obama waves during his speech in the House Chamber on Capitol Hill in Washington, D.C., February 24, 2009.

President Obama shares a copy of his address to a joint session of Congress with House Speaker Nancy Pelosi as Vice President Joe Biden applauds in the House Chamber on Capitol Hill in Washington, D.C., February 24, 2009.

POLARIS

submit will invest in the three areas that are absolutely critical to our economic future: energy, health care and education.

It begins with energy.

We know the country that harnesses the power of clean, renewable energy will lead the 21st century. And yet, it is China that has launched the largest effort in history to make their economy energy efficient. We invented solar technology, but we've fallen behind countries like Germany and Japan in producing it. New plug-in hybrids roll off our assembly lines, but they will run on batteries made in Korea.

Well I do not accept a future where the jobs and industries of tomorrow take root beyond our borders—and I know you don't either. It is time for America to lead again.

Thanks to our recovery plan, we will double this nation's supply of renewable energy in the next three years. We have also made the largest investment in basic research funding in American history—an investment that will spur not only new discoveries in energy, but breakthroughs in medicine, science and technology.

We will soon lay down thousands of miles of power lines that can carry new energy to cities and towns across this country. And we will put Americans to work making our homes and buildings more efficient so that we can save billions of dollars on our energy bills.

But to truly transform our economy, protect our security and save our planet from the ravages of climate change, we need to ultimately make clean, renewable energy the profitable kind of energy. So I ask this Congress to send me legislation that places a market-based cap on carbon pollution and drives the production of more renewable energy in America. And to support that innovation, we will invest $15 billion a year to develop technologies like wind power and solar power; advanced biofuels, clean coal, and more fuel-efficient cars and trucks built right here in America.

As for our auto industry, everyone recognizes that years of bad decision-making and a global recession have pushed our automakers to the brink. We should not, and will not, protect them from their own bad practices. But we are committed to the goal of a re-tooled, re-imagined auto industry that can compete and win. Millions of jobs depend on it. Scores of communities depend on it. And I believe the nation that invented the automobile cannot walk away from it.

None of this will come without cost, nor will it be easy. But this is America. We don't do what's easy. We do what is necessary to move this country forward.

For that same reason, we must also address the crushing cost of health care.

This is a cost that now causes a bankruptcy in America every 30 seconds. By the end of the year, it could cause 1.5 million Americans to lose their homes. In the last eight years, premiums have grown four times faster than wages. And in each of these years, one million more Americans have lost their health insurance. It is one of the major reasons why small businesses close their doors and corporations ship jobs overseas. And it's one of the largest and fastest-growing parts of our budget.

Given these facts, we can no longer afford to put health care reform on hold.

Already, we have done more to advance the cause of health care reform in the last 30 days than we have in the last decade. When it was days old, this Congress passed a law to provide and protect health insurance for 11 million American children whose parents work full-time. Our recovery plan will invest in electronic health records and new technology that will reduce errors, bring down costs, ensure privacy and save lives. It will launch a new effort to conquer a disease that has touched the life of nearly every American by seeking a cure for cancer in our time. And it makes the largest investment ever in preventive care, because that is one of the best ways to keep our people healthy and our costs under control.

This budget builds on these reforms. It includes an historic commitment to comprehensive health care reform—a downpayment on the principle that we must have quality, affordable health care for every American. It's a commitment that's paid for in part by efficiencies in our system that are long overdue. And it's a step we must take if we hope to bring down our deficit in the years to come.

Now, there will be many different opinions and ideas about how to achieve reform, and that is why I'm bringing together businesses and workers, doctors and health care providers, Democrats and Republicans to begin work on this issue next week.

I suffer no illusions that this will be an easy process. It will be hard. But I also know that nearly a century after Teddy Roosevelt first called for reform, the cost of our health care has weighed down our economy and the conscience of our nation long enough. So let there be no doubt: Health care reform cannot wait, it must not wait and it will not wait another year.

The third challenge we must address is the urgent need to expand the promise of education in America.

In a global economy where the most valuable skill you can sell is your knowledge, a good education is no longer just a pathway to opportunity—it is a prerequisite.

Right now, three-quarters of the fastest-growing occupations require more than a high school diploma. And yet, just over half of our citizens have that level of education. We have one of the highest high school dropout rates of any industrialized nation. And half of the students who begin college never finish.

This is a prescription for economic decline, because we know the countries that out-teach us today will out-compete us tomorrow. That is why it will be the goal of this administration to ensure that every child has access to a complete and competitive education—from the day they are born to the day they begin a career.

Already, we have made an historic investment in education through the economic recovery plan. We have dramatically expanded early childhood education and will continue to improve its quality, because we know that the most formative learning comes in those first years of life. We have made college affordable for nearly seven million more students. And we have provided the resources necessary to prevent painful cuts and teacher layoffs that would set back our children's progress.

But we know that our schools don't just need more resources. They need more reform. That is why this budget creates new incentives for teacher performance; pathways for advancement; and rewards for success. We'll invest in innovative programs that are already helping schools meet high standards and close achievement gaps. And we will expand our commitment to charter schools.

It is our responsibility as lawmakers and educators to make this system work. But it is the responsibility of every citizen to participate in it. And so tonight, I ask every American to commit to at least one year or more of higher education or career training. This can be community college or a four-year school; vocational training or an apprenticeship. But whatever the training may be, every American will need to get more than a high school diploma. And dropping out of high school is no longer an option. It's not just quitting on yourself, it's quitting on your country—and this country needs and values the talents of every American. That is why we will provide the support necessary for you to complete college and meet a new goal: By 2020, America will once again have the highest proportion of college graduates in the world.

I know that the price of tuition is higher than ever, which is why if you are willing to volunteer in your neighborhood or give back to your community or serve your country, we will make sure that you can afford a higher education. And to encourage a renewed spirit of national service for this and future generations, I ask this Congress to send me the bipartisan legislation that bears the name of Senator Orrin Hatch as well as an American who has never stopped asking what he can do for his country—Senator Edward Kennedy.

These education policies will open the doors of opportunity for our children. But it is up to us to ensure they walk through them. In the end, there is no program or policy that can substitute for a mother or father who will attend those parent/teacher conferences, or help with homework after dinner, or turn off the TV, put away the video games and read to their child. I speak to you not just as a President, but as a father when I say that responsibility for our children's education must begin at home.

There is, of course, another responsibility we have to our children. And that is the responsibility to ensure that we do not pass on to them a debt they cannot pay. With the deficit we inherited, the cost of the crisis we face and the long-term challenges we must meet, it has never been more important to ensure that as our economy recovers, we do what it takes to bring this deficit down.

I'm proud that we passed the recovery plan free of earmarks, and I want to pass a budget next year that ensures that each dollar we spend reflects only our most important national priorities.

Yesterday, I held a fiscal summit where I pledged to cut the deficit in half by the end of my first term in office. My administration has also begun to go line by line through the federal budget in order to eliminate wasteful and ineffective programs. As you can imagine, this is a process that will take some time. But we're starting with the biggest lines. We have already identified $2 trillion in savings over the next decade.

In this budget, we will end education programs that don't work and end direct payments to large agribusinesses that don't need them. We'll eliminate the no-bid contracts that have wasted billions in Iraq, and reform our defense budget so that we're not paying for Cold War-era weapons systems we don't use. We will root out the waste, fraud and abuse in our Medicare program that doesn't make our seniors any healthier, and we will restore a sense of fairness and balance to our tax code by finally ending the tax breaks for corporations that ship our jobs overseas.

In order to save our children from a future of debt, we will also end the tax breaks for the wealthiest 2% of Americans. But let me be perfectly clear, because I know you'll hear the same old claims that rolling back these tax breaks means a massive tax increase on the American people: If your family earns less than $250,000 a year, you will not see your taxes increased a single dime. I repeat: not one single dime. In fact, the recovery plan provides a tax cut—that's right, a tax cut—for 95% of working families. And these checks are on the way.

To preserve our long-term fiscal health, we must also address the growing costs in Medicare and Social Security. Comprehensive health care reform is the best way to strengthen Medicare for years to come. And we must also begin a conversation on how to do the same for Social Security, while creating tax-free universal savings accounts for all Americans.

Finally, because we're also suffering from a deficit of trust, I am committed to restoring a sense of honesty and accountability to our budget. That is why this budget looks ahead 10 years and accounts for spending that was left out under the old rules—and for the first time, that includes the full cost of fighting in Iraq and Afghanistan. For seven years, we have been a nation at war. No longer will we hide its price.

We are now carefully reviewing our policies in both wars, and I will soon announce a way forward in Iraq that leaves Iraq to its people and responsibly ends this war.

And with our friends and allies, we will forge a new and comprehensive strategy for Afghanistan and Pakistan to defeat al Qaeda and combat extremism. Because I will not allow terrorists to plot against the American people from safe havens half a world away.

As we meet here tonight, our men and women in uniform stand watch abroad and more are readying to deploy. To each and every one of them, and to the families who bear the quiet burden of their absence, Americans are united in sending one message: We honor your service, we are inspired by your sacrifice, and you have our unyielding support. To relieve the strain on our forces, my budget increases the number of our soldiers and Marines. And to keep our sacred trust with those who serve, we will raise their pay, and give our veterans the expanded health care and benefits that they have earned.

To overcome extremism, we must also be vigilant in upholding the values our troops defend—because there is no force in the world more powerful than the example of America. That is why I have ordered the closing of the detention center at Guantanamo Bay, and will seek swift and certain justice for captured terrorists—because living our values doesn't make us weaker, it makes us safer and it makes us stronger. And that is why I can stand here tonight and say without exception or equivocation that the United States of America does not torture.

In words and deeds, we are showing the world that a new era of engagement has begun. For we know that America cannot meet the threats of this century alone, but the world cannot meet them without America. We cannot shun the negotiating table, nor ignore the foes or forces that could do us harm. We are instead called to move forward with the sense of confidence and candor that serious times demand.

To seek progress toward a secure and lasting peace between Israel and her neighbors, we have appointed an envoy to sustain our effort. To meet the challenges of the 21st century—from terrorism to nuclear proliferation; from pandemic disease to cyber threats to crushing poverty—we will strengthen old alliances, forge new ones and use all elements of our national power.

And to respond to an economic crisis that is global in scope, we are working with the nations of the G20 to restore confidence in our financial system, avoid the possibility of escalating protectionism, and spur demand for American goods in markets across the globe. For the world depends on us to have a strong economy, just as our economy depends on the strength of the world's.

As we stand at this crossroads of history, the eyes of all people in all nations are once again upon us—watching to see what we do with this moment; waiting for us to lead.

Those of us gathered here tonight have been called to govern in extraordinary times. It is a tremendous burden, but also a great privilege—one that has been entrusted to few generations of Americans. For in our hands lies the ability to shape our world for good or for ill.

I know that it is easy to lose sight of this truth—to become cynical and doubtful; consumed with the petty and the trivial.

But in my life, I have also learned that hope is found in unlikely places; that inspiration often comes not from those with the most power or celebrity, but from the dreams and aspirations of Americans who are anything but ordinary.

I think about Leonard Abess, the bank president from Miami who reportedly cashed out of his company, took a $60 million bonus and gave it out to all 399 people who worked for him, plus another 72 who used to work for him. He didn't tell anyone, but when the local newspaper found out, he simply said, "I knew some of these people since I was 7 years old. I didn't feel right getting the money myself."

I think about Greensburg, Kansas, a town that was completely destroyed by a tornado, but is being rebuilt by its residents as a global example of how clean energy can power an entire community—how it can bring jobs and businesses to a place where piles of bricks and rubble once lay. "The tragedy was terrible," said one of the men who helped them rebuild. "But the folks here know that it also provided an incredible opportunity."

And I think about Ty'Sheoma Bethea, the young girl from that school I visited in Dillon, South Carolina—a place where the ceilings leak, the paint peels off the walls, and they have to stop teaching six times a day because the train barrels by their classroom. She has been told that her school is hopeless, but the other day after class she went to the public library and typed up a letter to the people sitting in this room. She even asked her principal for the money to buy a stamp. The letter asks us for help, and says, "We are just students trying to become lawyers, doctors, congressmen like yourself and one day president, so we can make a change to not just the state of South Carolina but also the world. We are not quitters."

We are not quitters.

These words and these stories tell us something about the spirit of the people who sent us here. They tell us that even in the most trying times, amid the most difficult circumstances, there is a generosity, a resilience, a decency and a determination that perseveres; a willingness to take responsibility for our future and for posterity.

Their resolve must be our inspiration. Their concerns must be our cause. And we must show them and all our people that we are equal to the task before us.

I know that we haven't agreed on every issue thus far, and there are surely times in the future when we will part ways. But I also know that every American who is sitting here tonight loves this country and wants it to succeed. That must be the starting point for every debate we have in the coming months, and where we return after those debates are done. That is the foundation on which the American people expect us to build common ground.

And if we do—if we come together and lift this nation from the depths of this crisis; if we put our people back to work and restart the engine of our prosperity; if we confront without fear the challenges of our time and summon that enduring spirit of an America that does not quit, then someday years from now, our children can tell their children that this was the time when we performed, in the words that are carved into this very chamber, "something worthy to be remembered." Thank you, God Bless you and may God Bless the United States of America.

"NO ONE HAS WRITTEN YOUR DESTINY FOR YOU"

On July 16, 2009, President Obama addressed the NAACP Convention in New York in a memorable speech that celebrated the organization's remarkable civil rights achievements over the past 100 years and offered hope in overcoming present day challenges

Thank you. What an extraordinary night, capping off an extraordinary week, capping off an extraordinary 100 years at the NAACP.

So Chairman Bond, Brother Justice, I am so grateful to all of you for being here. It's just good to be among friends.

It is an extraordinary honor to be here, in the city where the NAACP was formed, to mark its centennial. What we celebrate tonight is not simply the journey the NAACP has traveled, but the journey that we, as Americans, have traveled over the past 100 years.

It's a journey that takes us back to a time before most of us were born, long before the Voting Rights Act, and the Civil Rights Act, Brown v. Board of Education; back to an America just a generation past slavery. It was a time when Jim Crow was a way of life; when lynchings were all too common; when race riots were shaking cities across a segregated land.

It was in this America where an Atlanta scholar named W.E.B. Du Bois —a man of towering intellect and a fierce passion for justice, sparked what became known as the Niagara movement; where reformers united, not by color, but by cause; where an association was born that would, as its charter says, promote equality and eradicate prejudice among citizens of the United States.

From the beginning, these founders understood how change would come—just as King and all the civil rights giants did later. They understood that unjust laws needed to be overturned; that legislation needed to be passed; and that Presidents needed to be pressured into action. They knew that the stain of slavery and the sin of segregation had to be lifted in the courtroom, and in the legislature, and in the hearts and the minds of Americans.

They also knew that here, in America, change would have to come from the people. It would come from people protesting lynchings, rallying

President Obama waves during the closing night of the NAACP's 100th anniversary celebration in New York, July 16, 2009.

against violence, all those women who decided to walk instead of taking the bus, even though they were tired after a long day of doing somebody else's laundry, looking after somebody else's children. It would come from men and women of every age and faith, and every race and region—taking Greyhounds on Freedom Rides; sitting down at Greensboro lunch counters; registering voters in rural Mississippi, knowing they would be harassed, knowing they would be beaten, knowing that some of them might never return.

Because of what they did, we are a more perfect union. Because Jim Crow laws were overturned, black CEOs today run Fortune 500 companies. Because civil rights laws were passed, black mayors, black governors and members of Congress served in places where they might once have been able [sic] not just to vote but even take a sip of water. And because ordinary people did such extraordinary things, because they made the civil rights movement their own, even though there may not be a plaque or their names might not be in the history books—because of their efforts I made a little trip to Springfield, Illinois, a couple years ago—where Lincoln once lived, and race riots once raged—and began the journey that has led me to be here tonight as the 44th President of the United States of America.

Because of them I stand here tonight, on the shoulders of giants. And I'm here to say thank you to those pioneers and thank you to the NAACP.

And yet, even as we celebrate the remarkable achievements of the past 100 years; even as we inherit extraordinary progress that cannot be denied; even as we marvel at the courage and determination of so many plain folk—we know that too many barriers still remain.

We know that even as our economic crisis batters Americans of all races, African-Americans are out of work more than just about anybody else—a gap that's widening here in New York City, as a detailed report this week by Comptroller Bill Thompson laid out.

We know that even as spiraling health care costs crush families of all races, African-Americans are more likely to suffer from a host of diseases but less likely to own health insurance than just about anybody else.

We know that even as we imprison more people of all races than any nation in the world, an African-American child is roughly five times as likely as a white child to see the inside of a prison.

We know that even as the scourge of HIV/AIDS devastates nations abroad, particularly in Africa, it is devastating the African-American community here at home with disproportionate force. We know these things.

These are some of the barriers of our time. They're very different from the barriers faced by earlier generations. They're very different from the ones faced when fire hoses and dogs were being turned on young marchers; when Charles Hamilton Houston and a group of young Howard lawyers were dismantling segregation case by case across the land.

But what's required today—what's required to overcome today's barriers is the same as what was needed then. The same commitment. The same sense of urgency. The same sense of sacrifice. The same sense of community. The same willingness to do our part for ourselves and one another that has always defined America at its best and the African-American experience at its best.

And so the question is, where do we direct our efforts? What steps do we take to overcome these barriers? How do we move forward in the next 100 years?

The first thing we need to do is make real the words of the NAACP charter and eradicate prejudice, bigotry and discrimination among citizens of the United States. I understand there may be a temptation among some to think that discrimination is no longer a problem in 2009. And I believe that overall, there probably has never been less discrimination in America than there is today. I think we can say that.

But make no mistake: The pain of discrimination is still felt in America. By African-American women paid less for doing the same work as colleagues of a different color and a different gender. By Latinos made to feel unwelcome in their own country. By Muslim Americans viewed with suspicion simply because they kneel down to pray to their God. By our gay brothers and sisters, still taunted, still attacked, still denied their rights.

On the 45th anniversary of the Civil Rights Act, discrimination cannot stand—not on account of color or gender; how you worship or who you love. Prejudice has no place in the United States of America. That's what the NAACP stands for. That's what the NAACP will continue to fight for as long as it takes.

But we also know that prejudice and discrimination—at least the most blatant types of prejudice and discrimination—are not even the steepest barriers to opportunity today. The most difficult barriers include structural inequalities that our nation's legacy of discrimination has left behind; inequalities still plaguing too many communities and too often the object of national neglect.

These are barriers we are beginning to tear down one by one—by rewarding work with an expanded tax credit; by making housing more affordable; by giving ex-offenders a second chance. These are barriers we're targeting through our White House Office on Urban Affairs, through programs like Promise Neighborhoods that builds on Geoffrey Canada's success with the Harlem Children's Zone—that foster a comprehensive approach to ending poverty by putting all children on a pathway to college, and giving them the schooling and after-school support that they need to get there.

I think all of us understand that our task of reducing these structural inequalities has been made more difficult by the state and structure of our broader economy; an economy that for the last decade has been fueled by a cycle of boom and bust; an economy where the rich got really, really rich, but ordinary folks didn't see their incomes or their wages go up; an economy built on credit cards, shady mortgage loans; an economy built not on a rock, but on sand.

That's why my administration is working so hard not only to create and save jobs in the short-term, not only to extend unemployment insurance and help for people who have lost their health care in this crisis, not just to stem the immediate economic wreckage, but to lay a new foundation for growth and prosperity that will put opportunity within the reach of not just African-Americans, but all Americans. All Americans. Of every race. Of every creed. From every region of the country. We want everybody to participate in the American Dream. That's what the NAACP is all about.

Now, one pillar of this new foundation is health insurance for everybody. Health insurance reform that cuts costs and makes quality health

President Obama greets the audience at the NAACP's annual convention in New York, July 16, 2009.

SPENCER PLATT/GETTY IMAGES

coverage affordable for all, and it closes health care disparities in the process. Another pillar is energy reform that makes clean energy profitable, freeing America from the grip of foreign oil; putting young people to work upgrading low-income homes, weatherizing and creating jobs that can't be outsourced. Another pillar is financial reform with consumer protections to crackdown on mortgage fraud and stop predatory lenders from targeting black and Latino communities all across the country.

All these things will make America stronger and more competitive. They will drive innovation, they will create jobs, they will provide families with more security. And yet, even if we do all that, the African-American community will still fall behind in the United States and the United States will fall behind in the world unless we do a far better job than we have been doing of educating our sons and daughters.

I hope you don't mind—I want to go into a little detail here about education. In the 21st century—when so many jobs will require a bachelor's degree or more, when countries that out-educate us today will out-compete us tomorrow—a world-class education is a prerequisite for success.

There's no two ways about it. There's no way to avoid it. You know what I'm talking about. There's a reason the story of the civil rights movement was written in our schools. There's a reason Thurgood Marshall took up the cause of Linda Brown. There's a reason why the Little Rock Nine defied a governor and a mob. It's because there is no stronger weapon against inequality and no better path to opportunity than an education that can unlock a child's God-given potential.

And yet, more than half a century after Brown v. Board, the dream of a world-class education is still being deferred all across the country. African-American students are lagging behind white classmates in reading and math—an achievement gap that is growing in states that once led the way in the civil rights movement. Over half of all African-American students are dropping out of school in some places. There are overcrowded classrooms, and crumbling schools, and corridors of shame in America filled with poor children—not just black children, brown and white children as well.

The state of our schools is not an African-American problem; it is an American problem. Because if black and brown children cannot compete, then America cannot compete. And let me say this, if Al Sharpton, Mike Bloomberg and Newt Gingrich can agree that we need to solve the education problem, then that's something all of America can agree we can solve. Those guys came into my office. Just sitting in the Oval Office—I kept on doing a double-take. So that's a sign of progress and it is a sign of the urgency of the education problem. All of us can agree that we need to offer every child in this country—every child—

AUDIENCE: Amen!

THE PRESIDENT: Got an "Amen corner" back there—every child—every child in this country the best education the world has to offer from cradle through a career.

That's our responsibility as leaders. That's the responsibility of the United States of America. And we, all of us in government, have to work to do our part by not only offering more resources, but also demanding more reform. Because when it comes to education, we got to get past this whole paradigm, this outdated notion that somehow it's just money; or somehow it's just reform, but no money—and embrace what Dr. King called the "both-and" philosophy. We need more money, and we need more reform.

When it comes to higher education we're making college and advanced training more affordable, and strengthening community colleges that are the gateway to so many with an initiative—that will prepare students not only to earn a degree, but to find a job when they graduate; an initiative that will help us meet the goal I have set of leading the world in college degrees by 2020. We used to rank number one in college graduates. Now we are in the middle of the pack. And since we are seeing more and more African-American and Latino youth in our population, if we are leaving them behind we cannot achieve our goal, and America will fall further behind—and that is not a future that I accept and that is not a future that the NAACP is willing to accept.

We're creating a Race to the Top fund that will reward states and public school districts that adopt 21st century standards and assessments. We're creating incentives for states to promote excellent teachers and replace bad ones—because the job of a teacher is too important for us to accept anything less than the best.

We also have to explore innovative approaches such as those being pursued here in New York City; innovations like Bard High School Early College and Medgar Evers College Preparatory School that are challenging students to complete high school and earn a free associate's degree or college credit in just four years.

And we should raise the bar when it comes to early learning programs. It's not enough just to have a babysitter. We need our young people stimulated and engaged and involved. We need our folks—involved in child development to understand the latest science. Today, some early learning programs are excellent. Some are mediocre. And some are wasting what studies show are by far a child's most formative years.

That's why I've issued a challenge to America's governors: If you match the success of states like Pennsylvania and develop an effective model for early learning; if you focus reform on standards and results in early learning programs; if you demonstrate how you will prepare the lowest income children to meet the highest standards of success—then you can compete for an Early Learning Challenge Grant that will help prepare all our children to enter kindergarten all ready to learn.

So these are some of the laws we're passing. These are some of the policies we are enacting. We are busy in Washington. Folks in Congress are getting a little tuckered out. But I'm telling them—I'm telling them we can't rest, we've got a lot of work to do. The American people are counting on us. These are some of the ways we're doing our part in government to overcome the inequities, the injustices, the barriers that still exist in our country.

But all these innovative programs and expanded opportunities will not, in and of themselves, make a difference if each of us, as parents and as community leaders, fail to do our part by encouraging excellence in our children. Government programs alone won't get our children to the Promised Land. We need a new mindset, a new set of attitude—because one of the most durable and destructive legacies of discrimination is the way we've internalized a sense of limitation; how so many in our community have come to expect so little from the world and from themselves.

We've got to say to our children, yes, if you're African-American, the odds of growing up amid crime and gangs are higher. Yes, if you live in a poor neighborhood, you will face challenges that somebody in a wealthy suburb does not have to face. But that's not a reason to get bad grades—that's not a reason to cut class—that's not a reason to give up on your education and drop out of school. No one has written your destiny for you. Your destiny is in your hands—you cannot forget that. That's what we have to teach all of our children. No excuses. No excuses.

You get that education, all those hardships will just make you stronger, better able to compete. Yes we can.

To parents—to parents, we can't tell our kids to do well in school and then fail to support them when they get home. You can't just contract out parenting. For our kids to excel, we have to accept our responsibility to help them learn. That means putting away the Xbox—putting our kids to bed at a reasonable hour. It means attending those parent-teacher conferences and reading to our children and helping them with their homework.

And by the way, it means we need to be there for our neighbor's sons and daughters. We need to go back to the time, back to the day when we parents saw somebody, saw some kid fooling around and—it wasn't your child, but they'll whup you anyway. Or at least they'll tell your parents—the parents will. You know. That's the meaning of community. That's how we can reclaim the strength and the determination and the hopefulness that helped us come so far; helped us make a way out of no way.

It also means pushing our children to set their sights a little bit higher. They might think they've got a pretty good jump shot or a pretty good flow, but our kids can't all aspire to be LeBron or Lil' Wayne. I want them aspiring to be scientists and engineers—doctors and teachers—not just ballers and rappers. I want them aspiring to be a Supreme Court Justice. I want them aspiring to be the President of the United States of America.

I want their horizons to be limitless. I don't—don't tell them they can't do something. Don't feed our children with a sense of—that somehow because of their race that they cannot achieve.

Yes, government must be a force for opportunity. Yes, government must be a force for equality. But ultimately, if we are to be true to our past, then we also have to seize our own future, each and every day.

And that's what the NAACP is all about. The NAACP was not founded in search of a handout. The NAACP was not founded in search of favors. The NAACP was founded on a firm notion of justice; to cash the promissory note of America that says all of our children, all God's children, deserve a fair chance in the race of life.

It's a simple dream, and yet one that all too often has been denied—and is still being denied to so many Americans. It's a painful thing, seeing that dream denied. I remember visiting a Chicago school in a rough neighborhood when I was a community organizer, and some of the children gathered 'round me. And I remember thinking how remarkable it was that all of these children seemed so full of hope, despite being born into poverty, despite being delivered, in some cases, into addiction, despite all the obstacles they were already facing—you could see that spark in their eyes. They were the equal of children anywhere.

And I remember the principal of the school telling me that soon that sparkle would begin to dim, that things would begin to change; that soon, the laughter in their eyes would begin to fade; that soon, something would shut off inside, as it sunk in—because kids are smarter than we give them credit for—as it sunk in that their hopes would not come to pass—not because they weren't smart enough, not because they weren't talented enough, not because of anything about them inherently, but because, by accident of birth, they had not received a fair chance in life.

I know what can happen to a child who doesn't have that chance. But I also know what can happen to a child that does. I was raised by a single mom. I didn't come from a lot of wealth. I got into my share of trouble as a child. My life could have easily taken a turn for the worse. When I drive through Harlem or I drive through the South Side of Chicago, and I see young men on the corners, I say, there but for the grace of God go I. They're no less gifted than me. They're no less talented than me.

But I had some breaks. That mother of mine, she gave me love; she pushed me, she cared about my education; she took no lip; she taught me right from wrong. Because of her, I had a chance to make the most of my abilities. I had the chance to make the most of my opportunities. I had the chance to make the most of life.

The same story holds true for Michelle. The same story holds true for so many of you. And I want all the other Barack Obamas out there, and all the other Michelle Obamas out there—to have the same chance—the chance that my mother gave me; that my education gave me; that the United States of America has given me. That's how our union will be perfected and our economy rebuilt. That is how America will move forward in the next 100 years.

And we will move forward. This I know—for I know how far we have come. Some, you saw, last week in Ghana, Michelle and I took Malia and Sasha and my mother-in-law to Cape Coast Castle, in Ghana. Some of you may have been there. This is where captives were once imprisoned before being auctioned; where, across an ocean, so much of the African-American experience began.

We went down into the dungeons where the captives were held. There was a church above one of the dungeons—which tells you something about saying one thing and doing another. I was—we walked through the "Door Of No Return." I was reminded of all the pain and all the hardships, all the injustices and all the indignities on the voyage from slavery to freedom.

But I was reminded of something else. I was reminded that no matter how bitter the rod, how stony the road, we have always persevered. We have not faltered, nor have we grown weary. As Americans, we have demanded, and strived for, and shaped a better destiny. And that is what we are called on to do once more. NAACP, it will not be easy. It will take time. Doubts may rise, and hopes may recede.

But if John Lewis could brave Billy clubs to cross a bridge—then I know young people today can do their part and lift up our community.

If Emmet [sic] Till's uncle, Mose Wright, could summon the courage to testify against the men who killed his nephew, I know we can be better fathers and better brothers and better mothers and sisters in our own families.

If three civil rights workers in Mississippi—black, white, Christian and Jew, city-born and country-bred—could lay down their lives in freedom's cause, I know we can come together to face down the challenges of our own time. We can fix our schools—we can heal our sick, we can rescue our youth from violence and despair.

And 100 years from now, on the 200th anniversary of the NAACP—let it be said that this generation did its part; that we too ran the race; that full of faith that our dark past has taught us, full of the hope that the present has brought us—we faced, in our lives and all across this nation, the rising sun of a new day begun.

Thank you. God Bless you. God Bless the United States of America.

PETE SOUZA/THE WHITE HOUSE/GETTY IMAGES